Jasmin Paris Biography

The Remarkable Odyssey of a Trailblazing Skyrunner and Barkley Marathons Victor

Curtis A. Claud

Copyright © 2024 by Curtis A. Claud

All rights reserved. No part of this publication may be reproduced, distributed, or transmitted in any form or by any means, including photocopying, recording, or other electronic or mechanical methods, without the prior written permission of the publisher, except in the case of brief quotations embodied in critical reviews and certain other noncommercial uses permitted by copyright law.

Table of Contents

Chapter 1: Beginnings: From Manchester to the Peak District..................................5

Chapter 2: University, Outdoor Adventures, and the Beginning of a Running Journey........9

Chapter 3: Conquering the Peaks: Triumphs, Records, and Championship Titles............... 13

Chapter 4: Breaking Boundaries: Shift to Ultra Distance Running and Global Triumph..17

Chapter 5: Ascending New Heights and Making History................................ 21

Chapter 6: Barkley Marathons: A Daunting Test and a Landmark Achievement.............. 26

Chapter 7: Stabilizing Running with Personal Life and Academic... 31

Conclusion... 35

Chapter 1: Beginnings: From Manchester to the Peak District

Jasmin Paris's path to becoming a pioneering athlete started in the vibrant city of Manchester, where she was born in November 1983. Growing up in a family that emphasized both education and adventure, her early life set the stage for her future pursuits in the outdoors. Although Manchester was an urban environment, her parents cultivated in her a love for nature and physical activity.

As a young girl, Paris often sought peace in nature, escaping the city's fast pace by exploring the green spaces that dotted Manchester. Whether roaming local parks or venturing into the surrounding countryside, she developed a deep connection to the outdoors. These early encounters with nature sparked a passion for adventure and running that would shape her future. However, it was the wild beauty of the Peak District, just outside of Manchester, where Paris's love for the outdoors truly flourished. With its vast moorlands, rocky landscapes, and winding trails, the Peak District National Park became her playground for exploration and discovery.

From an early age, Paris was captivated by the challenge of the rugged terrain. Accompanied by her family, she spent many weekends hiking, camping, and immersing herself in the area's natural wonders. These experiences instilled a sense of curiosity and wonder, fueling a lifelong passion for outdoor adventure.

As she grew older, Paris sought more demanding adventures within the Peak District. She eagerly tackled harder routes and tested her physical endurance against the unforgiving landscape. Whether scaling cliffs, navigating tricky paths, or braving unpredictable weather, each challenge only deepened her love for the outdoors and her determination to push her limits. It was in these formative years that Paris discovered her love for running.

Drawn to the sense of freedom and excitement that came from running on trails, she embraced the sport as a way to connect with nature. Each run brought a sense of empowerment and exhilaration, driving her to go further and faster. By the time she reached her teenage years, Paris had developed into a gifted runner with a fierce competitive spirit. She began participating in local races, testing her abilities against other runners. Despite facing strong competition, she quickly made a name for herself, setting the stage for even greater athletic achievements in the future. Looking back at Jasmin Paris's early years in Manchester and the Peak District, it's clear that her upbringing profoundly influenced her life's trajectory. Her childhood adventures in nature and discovery of a passion for running laid the groundwork for her future success as a trailblazing athlete.

Chapter 2: University, Outdoor Adventures, and the Beginning of a Running Journey

Jasmin Paris's transformation from university student to elite athlete showcases her unwavering commitment, passion for adventure, and drive for excellence. Her time at the University of Liverpool marked the beginning of her love for the outdoors and the foundation for her remarkable career in running.

As an undergraduate, Paris was drawn to the dynamic atmosphere and community spirit at the University of Liverpool. She quickly connected with others who shared her enthusiasm for exploration and adventure, immersing herself in a world of outdoor possibilities. It was here that

Paris discovered the Open Air Club, a student group devoted to outdoor activities and fostering camaraderie. Excited by the chance to explore the natural beauty surrounding the university, she joined the club and embarked on a series of thrilling outdoor adventures.

Guided by experienced outdoor enthusiasts, Paris embraced activities like hiking, rock climbing, kayaking, and orienteering. Each new challenge brought her a sense of freedom and exhilaration, fueling her desire to push her boundaries. However, it was during a demanding trail run through the rugged Peak District that Paris found her true calling in running. The sense of liberation and empowerment she experienced navigating the trails on foot captivated her, and she quickly dedicated herself to becoming a distance runner.

Though she entered competitive running later than many, Paris rapidly made her presence felt. Her natural athletic ability, coupled with determination and focus, allowed her to rise quickly in the local racing circuit, earning a reputation as a fierce competitor on the trails.

During this period, Paris laid the foundation for her future as a groundbreaking athlete. Motivated by a desire to test her limits, she set ambitious goals and pursued them with relentless determination. Balancing her academic work with an increasingly rigorous training schedule, Paris's love for running only deepened. Each race fueled her passion, and the promise of new challenges spurred her forward. By the time she graduated from the University of Liverpool, Paris had established herself as one of the most promising young distance runners. With her sights set on even greater achievements, she embarked on the next phase of her journey with the focus and resolve that would eventually lead her to the top of her sport.

Chapter 3: Conquering the Peaks: Triumphs, Records, and Championship Titles

In the harsh, unforgiving landscape of the fells, Jasmin Paris rose to prominence, becoming a dominant figure with a string of victories, record-breaking performances, and championship titles. Her unmatched athletic prowess, steely determination, and drive for excellence made her one of the most formidable forces in the world of fell running.

Paris's rise to the top was marked by an array of extraordinary wins, each showcasing her endurance, tenacity, and exceptional talent. Whether it was the renowned Three Peaks Race or the grueling courses of Wasdale, Borrowdale,

Langdale Horseshoe, Ennerdale Horseshoe, and Isle of Jura, Paris conquered the most challenging terrain in the UK with apparent ease, solidifying her reputation as an unstoppable competitor. Her prowess extended beyond individual races to championship competitions, where she consistently outperformed her rivals, earning major titles year after year.

Highlights of her career included back-to-back victories at the Scottish Hill Running Championships in 2014 and 2015, and wins in the British Fell Running Championships in 2015 and 2018, cementing her place among the sport's elite. Paris's true mastery of the fells became evident when she ventured into ultra-distance events. In 2015, she began transitioning from shorter races to longer, more demanding challenges, pushing her limits even further. Her record-breaking feat at the Fellsman, where she set a new women's record of 11:09 and placed fourth overall, marked her rise in ultra running. Her crowning achievement came in 2016 when she demolished the women's record for the Bob Graham Round, completing the iconic route in an astonishing 15:24. Her relentless pace and drive earned her widespread recognition, cementing her legacy in fell running history.

Paris's quest for greatness didn't stop there. In 2016, she tackled the Ramsay Round, completing the daunting course in 16:13, setting not only a new women's record but also the fastest known time overall. This stunning performance solidified her reputation as one of the greatest fell runners of her time, earning admiration from fans and competitors alike. Jasmin Paris's dominance in fell running wasn't a product of luck but the result of years of dedication, sacrifice, and an unwavering commitment to excellence. From her early days as a rising talent to her record-shattering achievements on the toughest courses, her story is a powerful testament to the impact of perseverance, passion, and the pursuit of greatness.

Chapter 4: Breaking Boundaries: Shift to Ultra Distance Running and Global Triumph

Jasmin Paris's transition from dominating fell races to excelling in ultra distance running marked a significant turning point in her career, propelling her to global recognition and affirming her as one of the most exceptional endurance athletes.

With unmatched determination, remarkable stamina, and an insatiable drive for success, Paris embraced new challenges, conquering some of the world's toughest races and earning widespread admiration. Her foray into ultra running began in 2015, as Paris sought to push her physical and mental limits in longer, more punishing races. Motivated by a desire to go beyond traditional races, she embarked on an ambitious quest to explore the extremes of her capabilities. One of her earliest ultra-distance achievements was in the Fellsman, a 61-mile race through the demanding Yorkshire Dales.

Despite being new to ultra running, Paris immediately made a significant impact, setting a new women's record of 11:09 and finishing fourth overall. This stellar performance captured the attention of the ultra running community, establishing her as a rising talent. Paris's true breakthrough came later that year when she competed in the Dragon's Back Race, a five-day endurance challenge across the treacherous mountains of Wales. Known as one of the hardest multi-day races globally, it tests even the most seasoned runners. Paris, undeterred by the intense competition and brutal conditions, demonstrated extraordinary resilience. Over five relentless days, she overcame fatigue, injuries, and the harsh Welsh weather to secure a historic finish as the first female and second overall, solidifying her place among the world's top ultrarunners.

Her momentum continued into 2019, when Paris made history by becoming the first woman to win the Spine Race, a brutal 268-mile journey along the Pennine Way. Battling extreme weather, sleep deprivation, and exhaustion, she crossed the finish line in a record-setting 83 hours, 12 minutes, and 23 seconds, further cementing her legendary status. Paris's international accomplishments underscored her standing as a world-class ultrarunner. In 2016, she took third place in the ultra category at the

Skyrunning World Championships, showcasing her adaptability on the global stage. Later that year, she competed in the prestigious Ultra-Trail du Mont-Blanc (UTMB), her first 100-mile race, finishing an impressive sixth and demonstrating her exceptional endurance against elite global competition. Jasmin Paris's journey into ultra distance running and her international triumphs reflect years of relentless dedication and perseverance. From her early days in the fells to her record-breaking performances in the world's most demanding ultra races, Paris's story is one of passion, resilience, and an unwavering pursuit of excellence.

Chapter 5: Ascending New Heights and Making History

Jasmin Paris's entry into the thrilling realm of skyrunning marked a significant evolution in her impressive career, pushing her endurance limits and highlighting her athletic versatility. With exceptional athletic prowess, steadfast determination, and a courageous spirit, she triumphed in some of the most challenging mountain races globally, accumulating numerous victories and setting new records.

Skyrunning, which blends aspects of mountain running, trail running, and alpinism, presented Paris with fresh challenges and opportunities to stretch her capabilities. Unlike conventional trail races, skyrunning events feature steep climbs, technical descents, and high-altitude conditions, making them among the most demanding competitions worldwide. Paris's serious engagement with skyrunning began in 2016, as she targeted the Skyrunner World Series—a prestigious circuit of mountain races that draws elite competitors from across the globe. With her characteristic grit and resolve, she quickly made her mark, earning recognition as a leading contender in the series.

A standout moment in her skyrunning career came in 2016 when she secured victory in the Sky Extreme category of the Skyrunner World Series. Competing against some of the sport's fiercest rivals, she skillfully navigated challenging terrain, dizzying heights, and harsh weather conditions, establishing herself as a pioneer in skyrunning. Her performance at the

Skyrunning World Championships later that year further highlighted her prowess on the global stage. Competing in the ultra category, she claimed the bronze medal, solidifying her reputation as one of the leading skyrunners worldwide and earning the admiration of fans and competitors alike. Paris's accomplishments in skyrunning extended beyond individual races and championships.

She also demonstrated her competitive edge in some of the sport's most iconic events, including the Buff Epic Trail 105K and the UTMB, where she finished sixth in her debut 100-mile race. Perhaps the pinnacle of Paris's skyrunning achievements occurred in 2024 when she became the first woman to successfully complete the Barkley Marathons, renowned as one of the most grueling and enigmatic races on the planet.

23

Hosted annually in Frozen Head State Park, Tennessee, the Barkley Marathons is infamous for its harsh terrain, unpredictable weather, and strict time constraints, making it an extraordinarily challenging event. Confronted with formidable obstacles and stiff competition, Paris met the challenge with her usual determination and resilience, conquering the course in a time of 59 hours, 58 minutes, and 21 seconds—just 99 seconds under the cutoff limit.

This historic accomplishment garnered international attention and solidified her position as one of the greatest skyrunners of her generation. Reflecting on Jasmin Paris's journey into skyrunning and her exceptional international success, it's evident that her achievements stem from years of commitment, sacrifice, and an unwavering drive to excel. From her early beginnings as a promising athlete to her record-setting performances on some of the world's toughest courses, Paris's story is a powerful testament to perseverance, passion, and an unyielding quest for excellence.

Chapter 6: Barkley Marathons: A Daunting Test and a Landmark Achievement

The Barkley Marathons epitomizes human endurance, resilience, and an unyielding spirit of adventure. Located in the challenging landscape of Frozen Head State Park in Tennessee, this enigmatic event has gained notoriety as one of the most arduous and mysterious ultramarathons globally.

Characterized by its punishing landscape, erratic weather, and rigorous time constraints, the Barkley Marathons presents a daunting challenge to even the most experienced athletes, demanding they push their physical and mental limits in the pursuit of achievement. The race originated in 1986, conceived by ultrarunner Gary Cantrell, known as "Lazarus Lake." He envisioned a contest that would push the boundaries of human endurance, drawing inspiration from the audacious escape of James Earl Ray from the nearby Brushy Mountain State Penitentiary.

Cantrell designed a course that wound through the rugged hills and valleys of Frozen Head State Park, requiring participants to navigate unmarked trails, steep ascents, and harsh descents. Since its creation, the Barkley Marathons has been cloaked in mystery, with its distance, elevation change, and route varying annually. Competitors must complete five laps of the course, each approximately 20 miles long, within a strict 60-hour time frame. With only a few scattered aid stations and no course markers, participants must depend on their navigation skills, endurance, and sheer will to finish the race. Throughout the years, the Barkley Marathons has solidified its reputation as one of the most grueling races worldwide, with only a small number of runners successfully completing it. The relentless terrain, extreme weather, and rigid time limits present a genuine test of endurance, pushing athletes to their physical and mental extremes while forcing them to confront their innermost fears and uncertainties.

In March 2022, Jasmin Paris joined the ranks of those who dared to challenge the Barkley Marathons, embarking on a journey that would test her limits in unimaginable ways. With her characteristic grit, determination, and unwavering focus, she aimed to conquer the course and become the first woman to complete the Barkley Marathons successfully. From the beginning, Paris encountered significant obstacles and fierce competition, with the harsh terrain and unpredictable conditions continuously threatening her progress. Nevertheless, she remained undeterred, driving herself to the edge of exhaustion as she fought through the grueling course, one mile at a time.

As hours turned into days and the distance stretched indefinitely, Paris's resolve never faltered. Each step brought her closer to her goal, fueled by the knowledge that she was on the verge of making history and earning her place among ultrarunning legends. In the early hours of the third day, Paris crossed the finish line in an astonishing time of 59 hours, 58 minutes, and 21 seconds—just 99 seconds before the cut-off. This landmark achievement garnered worldwide attention and solidified her status as one of the premier ultrarunners of her generation.

Chapter 7: Stabilizing Running with Personal Life and Academic

Jasmin Paris's extraordinary accomplishments as an ultrarunner reflect not only her exceptional athletic talent but also her skill in harmonizing the rigors of running with her academic and personal responsibilities. As a small-animal veterinarian and senior lecturer at the Royal (Dick) School of Veterinary Studies at the University of Edinburgh, she adeptly manages a demanding career alongside her intensive training routine, all while nurturing a family and pursuing her love for adventure.

From the very beginning of her running journey, Paris has shown an unwavering dedication to achieving excellence both on the trails and in her professional life. Despite the pressures of her academic and professional duties, she has successfully carved out time for training, competition, and outdoor exploration, all while remaining deeply committed to her studies and research.

A significant factor in Paris's success is her ability to efficiently allocate her time and prioritize her responsibilities. Her busy routine, which encompasses teaching, research, clinical practice, and administrative tasks, requires meticulous planning, organization, and self-discipline to ensure she can balance her running with her academic and family obligations. More crucial than effective time management, however, is Paris's enduring passion and commitment to both her running and her profession. For her, running transcends being merely a hobby; it is an integral part of her identity. It offers her a sense of purpose, fulfillment, and joy that enhances every facet of her life, both on the trails and beyond. In addition to her professional endeavors, Paris devotes quality time to her family, including her husband, Konrad Rawlik, and their two children.

Despite the challenges of raising a family while managing a demanding career and training schedule, she embraces parenthood with the same resolve and dedication that she applies to her running, aiming to provide her children with love, support, and encouragement as they pursue their own journeys in life. Paris's ability to integrate her running with her academic and personal life exemplifies her resilience, ingenuity, and steadfast commitment to excellence. Her journey serves as a reminder that with dedication, determination, and a focus on what truly matters, achieving balance is possible, both on the trails and in everyday life.

Conclusion

Paris's journey as an athlete, scholar, and mother exemplifies the power of determination, passion, and the unwavering pursuit of excellence. From her modest beginnings in Manchester to her groundbreaking victories on some of the world's most challenging trails, she has garnered admiration from fans and fellow competitors alike, leaving behind a legacy of shattered records and extraordinary accomplishments.

Reflecting on Paris's inspiring path reveals that her influence reaches far beyond the realm of running. She embodies more than just athletic prowess; she is a trailblazer, a pioneer, and a role model for aspiring athletes and adventurers. Her remarkable ability to harmonize her athletic endeavors with her academic and personal responsibilities showcases her resilience, creativity, and steadfast dedication to excellence. Even more commendable than Paris's athletic feats is her deep commitment to her family. Amid the demands of her career and training, she prioritizes her roles as a wife and mother, offering love, support, and encouragement to her husband and children as they face life's challenges together.

As her legacy continues to flourish, Paris remains devoted to pushing the limits of what is achievable both on the trails and in life. Whether setting records in the rugged Peak District, excelling in skyrunning, or balancing her parental duties with her academic and professional responsibilities, she tackles every challenge with the same determination, grit, and unwavering resolve that have characterized her career. However, Paris's journey is far from complete. With her sights set on new challenges, she remains ambitious and driven, eager to reach new heights of accomplishment. Whether she is preparing for her next ultramarathon, engaging in groundbreaking veterinary research, or cherishing time with her family, one thing is certain: Jasmin Paris will continue to inspire and astonish us with her remarkable feats for years to come.

Paris's story is a powerful illustration of perseverance, passion, and the relentless pursuit of excellence. From her early days as a promising young athlete to her historic wins on some of the toughest trails globally, she has navigated numerous obstacles to establish herself as one of the most formidable athletes of her generation. Yet, her unwavering dedication to her family and her commitment to living a balanced and meaningful life are perhaps even more impressive. As she continues to challenge the limits of possibility both on and off the trail, it is clear that Jasmin Paris's legacy will inspire athletes and adventurers around the globe for generations to come.

Printed in Great Britain
by Amazon